# MY HEART BLOWN OPEN WIDE

# MY HEART BLOWN OPEN WIDE

**Martin J. White**

Swansea
Hafan Books
2005

ISBN 0954514726

Published by Hafan Books                    First Impression 2005

Hafan Books is a non-profit publisher associated with Swansea Bay Asylum Seekers Support Group. SBASSG is a community group run by asylum seekers, refugees and other local people. All profits from Hafan Books publications go to SBASSG.

**Hafan Books** and **SBASSG** c/o
**The Retreat**
**2 Humphrey Street**
**SWANSEA**
**SA1 6BG**

Website: **www. hafan.org**

E-mail: **hafanbooks@yahoo.co.uk**

Printed in Wales by Gwasg Gomer

Layout by Martin White and Tom Cheesman

Cover designed by Martin White and Thomas Newton

Back cover photo by Louise Johnson

**Thanks to:**

Writers' groups in Huddersfield and Swansea

Amanda, Paul, Kate, Noah, Zaineb, Rhian, Carly, Emma, Karen, Kirsty, Taj and all at the Monkey Café

Nigel and Hazel at The Retreat

Mike Shields, Brendan Cleary, Jeffrey Wheatley, Roger Elkin, Sarah Wolloff, Martine Stead, Russell Bowley, Paul Canning, Milner Place, Stephanie Bowgett, John Duffy, Gary Hanson, Betty Blackburn, Sharon Sulman, Basil Morris, Ruth S. Davies, Stephanie Latham, Paul Parsons, David Woolley and Jim Gourlay

Special thanks to Tom Cheesman and Dafydd Wyn

**Dedications:**

'delicate' is for Debbie Brookes
'Indebted' is for Heulwen Davies
'learning' is for Julia Hall
'Virago' (OED Definition 2: 'Heroic woman') is for Paula Harries
'August night at the Monkey Café' is for Deb Hill
'opening' is for Karen Maddock-Jones
'not luck' is for George Knell
'Wendy's Book' is for Wendy Larcombe
'Life study' is for Amanda Maria
'taking flight' and 'for saousen' are for Saousen Ben Achour Mata
'Nightwalk' is for Dylan Murphy
'Nirvana' is for Maria Owen
'Way of the road' is for Sharon Sulman
'chink' is for Keiko Tanaka
'La Gioconda' is for Siân Taylor
'Eye candy' is for Anita Vukomanovic
'trusting' is for Saramea Waterman

**Credo:**

Without hope
to endure
without love
to be loving

To


Richard Smith


the most patient and considerate friend
a man could hope for

# CONTENTS

### Subterfuge

*I want to do sweet things for you*
*but have them seem like nothing*
*Cook superb meals*
*to make your stomach my ally*
*Present perfume as a way*
*of putting you off the scent*
*Buy you sandals not showing*
*I long to be there when you wear them*
*on a chic promenade*
*in sweltering summer*
*Get you a coat*
*without making it obvious*
*I'll want to see you wrapped in it*
*autumn and winter*
*Talk about work*
*travel*
*and next year*
*while letting you think*
*it's you that feels*
*we could build a wonderful future*
*Give you my heart*
*and hope you don't notice*

14

# WENDY'S BOOK

"no excuses, i won't apologise, or justify your lies
come and find me, tell them to me, look me in the eyes"

– Robbie Williams

## wendy

when earth is a blue memory
in the eye of a red giant
or we're no longer even ash
flecking a drop of spilt milk
diffuse, anonymous swirl
on an old path
                    and pattern printed
in dark fabric of space

where there's neither restlessness
nor rest, no witness
and loving voice
to link your diminutives
with my plain, distinguished name

once being one
                    will still be true
who joined, mouth and hip
but touched souls
time serene, irrevocable
that distant moment when we loved
bright as the birth of a star

**out of the blue**

with a wide blue void
to voyage
complete world of sky
in which to adventure
and escape
something holds them here

made of snow and sunlight
serene graceful gulls
with crocus-yellow bills
they turn or tumble    content

while others disappear
drift over horizons
of our hazy summer dreams
to return with winter
these linger    for a lifetime
at a minor river mouth

i was wanderer    not stayer
restless and reaching
for what shimmered
seemed meaningful
only as it slipped away

till taking a place
among bright white birds
in silent row along a railing
facing sea and bitter wind
no longer looking
i found love

**not a star**

except in my sky
or young
as she hoped
sometimes to seem
lines starting
from shy
bold eyes let you see
her love of laughter
and life
hasn't always been kind

clothes reserved
subdued organic colours
little
easily missed in a crowd
skin freckled and moly
hair longer
shorter
loosely gathered
or let fall beside her face
unstyled and flyaway

she rose
through darkness
and silence
heartening smile
golden over prospects
lifted a voice
love more powerful
than ever dreamt
was in me

## Beginning

Working together, we were green and sunny
as leaves, unknowingly perfect. Becoming
part of forest's old pattern, ever growing
self-sustaining, purposeful. Here to study

humble moss abounding with tiny creatures
scan high-lit canopies for a butterfly
purple and silver, but elusive. Tasks dry
scientific, formed bonds, suggested pleasures

a shared future of budding and belonging.
Opening as ferns do, imperceptibly
unstoppable; touched by some pollinating

spark, our little time of loving had begun
free to flourish, by a curiosity
of nature's kind accounting: two can be one.

## simple

you could wander slowly from a keeping curve
broad, bird-pebbled beach to near hilltops
patched purple brown with brooding heath
through lively Sandfields
Singleton contradicted by walkers
cyclists, playful dogs and children

look in bustling offices, factories, shops
stand at doors, a rainbow in rows of houses
neglecting no garden, albeit humble
note each soft face and softer
with utmost care

searching till sure you've seen everyone tender
and among them one so gentle
finding her, your heart forgot to beat

smile that's spring sunrise
dawn of hope to another heart
in a plain room, opulent feeling
or on the busiest street, a curious stillness
only when certain she's gentlest

you'll be looking at my love

## Pressing

Sat at back
of a meeting become boring
abstracted
from speaker and audience
guilty schoolkids
a combined age of seventy
we smiled a sidelong smile
began to touch hands
My fingers slowly stroking
little pillows of your palm
yours sliding upwards
inside mine
from root to tingling tip
gently pushing and pressing
Sharing a smouldering look
both sighed
Conference continued
We were an hour by car
from home
My mind recalled
complete relationships
that weren't as thrilling

**imagine**

two leaves
me and you
lifted toward light
but one green stem

overarching weather
a time of rain
absorbed as pulsing sap

hearing first song
from a high branch
aware of gorging chicks
hidden amongst thorns

summers grown into
winters patiently outwaited
for our moment

of blossoming
elated so admired
you and me
human forest rose-tree

## happy

dancing round with a duster
making furniture shine
waltzing a hoover along
laughing and feeling fine
my heart is beating faster
my girl is coming soon
reeling over red rooftops
this moon's a different moon

tangoing with a tea-towel
making crockery gleam
shimmying into clean clothes
living a lucid dream
my mind sees things so clearly
life makes sense since she came
whirling outside my window
these stars are not the same

## Fast food

Discovered this three-minute pasta
a recipe not in the book
tomato and olive pour-over sauce
for people too busy to cook

Heart-warming food for cold winter days
downed with a glass or two of red
so we could spend more time working outdoors
(and spend more time in bed)

**carrying**

to think you were once invisible
a chemical reaction    dividing cell
nebula spiralling slowly in starless dark
genes unfolding and ramifying
into plankton    into shrimp
becoming a curious fish
with fluttering    functioning gills
swimming serenely in amniotic ocean
and later, more complex    a cosmonaut
walking weightless in space
trailing a lifeline
linkage to your mother-ship
magical things to have been
before you were even born

but in that primal vastness    not alone
soon swaying face to face
in silent, mirrored dance
amazing with an identical twin
holding her in beginning arms
touching with unformed hands
till you had neat toes and fingers
tiny    haloed nails
began to smile    stood on your head
ready to enter this world

tonight    damp and dreaming
you're curled again
between this chest    these hips
and feeling you inside me
starts exactly that wide-eyed wonder
sense of cradling the future
as a new mother    when her child
fills the horizon    turning in her womb

## Giving

Let others lead, achieve, win undying fame
my agenda's full. Needed by a hurt girl
I've nothing for their 'nine-to-five', but unfurl
strengths, talents – and hopes – long withheld from a game

called 'life', that hell of elbowing and trampling.
To help re-ignite tall flames of self-esteem
see a sun of pride and belief in her dream
future light confident eyes; my work: loving

who gave me new and better reasons to live.
Re-connected, creating, a redemption
through shared purpose. Now I want only to give

everything: should circumstance break us apart
she'll know my love never faltered, this passion
to be no-one; but a good man in her heart.

## Conspirators

Arabesque motif, blue and white, you settle
pattern my rug, facing balcony and sunlight
miles away, tapping at your laptop
papers strewn round you. I sit upright
on a sofa studying 'The Failure of Psychiatry'
courageous truth-telling by a friend of mine.
Or trying to. Every so often you stop
lift a thoughtful face toward French doors
light catching in brimming eyes.
Unconsciously lowering this book
my look slides down a deep bend of back
raised on elbows; dainty petal feet
in mid-air, languidly crossing, re-crossing
those comfortable 'go-faster' striped leggings
tight over curves divinely cleft.
And you catch me looking, shoot me
a knowing smile and make me smile.
Concentrating, clock a glazed-eyed chaperone
to lull asleep while plotting more pleasure
recalling stars we touched an hour ago
your eyes say will soon fall again.

**ivory tower**

somewhere
south of here
people are starving
but
though considered poor
i can always eat

somewhere
further east
people are fighting and dying
victims of a violence
we call civilisation
but
it's an image on tv
here i feel safe

to west and north
other cruelties
and hungers
i could see dramatised
but
don't have to face

everywhere
round the compass
people are lonely
but
i'm with you
and have no needs

**love**

to wake beside her
see her smile
before anything else

sit up in bed    me with a coffee
her with a cup of tea
and plan our day

her toothbrush
next to my toothbrush
small boots    alongside mine
as we dress for work

spend hours
raking cut bracken
or thinning sycamore
intent and careful
but never ceasing
to be aware    of her nearby

down tools    at day's end
laugh    with friends in a pub
our eyes    meeting
now and then
finally to be home

to bathe    and eat together
feel her fit
neatly under my chin
as she comes into my arms

such a pull
and power in all of it
what is
the word for that?

## zenith

elsewhere
billionaires checking balance-sheets
became trillionaires
power-hungry politicians were re-elected
trophy wives and husbands paraded for the paparazzi
gorgeously preened
plantations of marijuana were smoked
and pyramids of cocaine snorted

while millions of people
a little more like us
packed pubs with raucous noise
but laughter
and conga'd at midnight

as a new year was born
we stayed at home
ate a roast dinner
drank whisky and canada dry
meant love and made it
stood by a window
watching fireworks climb a clear sky
and no-one on earth was happier

## numb

trees are flat
stiff as a backdrop
stunned by loss of their leaves

clean ice hummocks
hint of coming floes
swans drift bewildered and mute

sunless sky blank and stifled
clouds banded
dull and duller grey

a turned tide ebbs    slow as time

no longer eating
sleeping breathing    human
not yet in pain
i linger at a window
nothing happening inside or out

in a shell seeming insulated
from crack and inrush
but imperceptibly sinking
through infinite sadness

you're lost to me
and days have no tempo
clocks without hands

somewhere perhaps
springs are compressed
cogs engage    flywheels spin

clouds will    somehow
slide down sky

sea return    to break
again and again

## petrel

come at last to land
she'd rested a weary heart
let me care and nestled close
though suggesting    fatefully
round-eyed fretting
of an oiled    cornered bird

limitless    my new feeling
fierce to lift and love
cleanse from her silkiness
a clingy scum of wrong
found an enfolding use
for these ungainly limbs

but sound and sure again
she seeks some shape or space
felt as a larger life
part of a bold nature    pushing her
to go where hurts are found

as if to be fully alive
she must be far
from help or haven
alone    between sea and sky
testing slight strength
against a storm    flying in face
of bullying bluster

wanting her to stay
unwilling to hold her back
i watch her try wings

## To break free

Soft brightness of nascent year
filtered through whispering firs

We stood invisible, beaten, at bay
screened from cold breeze
sunwarmed, your hair flowing
silk across my skin, faces pressed
close, hot, arms holding tight
our muscle, nerves, bone and blood

No end of me, beginning of you
one heart, but heavy
a deep and final harmony, grieving
over sadness that had come

Mesmeric, magical being
in your occult element there
you might wordless wish, summon
a merciful spirit of that place
could make a charm to hold us
fused by love's melding heat
into single, seamless trunk
and graceful limbs of generic tree
obscure among mirror kin
beyond pursuit or harm

Happier to stand, raising arms
always skyward, never tiring
and bend with the wind, forget
to be parted by human delusions

Start spring, flame with autumn
one sap and fibre
absorbed in nature's purpose
a modest, carefree happiness
that couldn't be taken from us

Without regret
relinquish aching heart and mind
exhausted human form

## Possession

For early humans, an eclipse of chilled sun
silencing earth, portended famine or doom
and when over our life he began to loom
– claiming ownership, bullying, heartless one

you'd said was obsessed, but had never seemed real –
I felt instinctual fear, readiness to fight.
Our love appeared strong, him a mere satellite
yet had pull you were unable to conceal:

though hating his mind games and cold mistreatment
urged by me, true friends, an anxious family
you couldn't flout gravity, never got free.

So a cruel, creeping darkness had to be faced
stealing warmth, laughter, too selfish to relent
and our peaceful, unfettered world was laid waste.

## Orion

Behind blue camouflage, unseen
crossing mythless, unpeopled skies
to crouch below sunset's last horizon
wait for night and ambush

ones proving always beyond reach
so merely stand sentinel, not drawing
from spangled sheath a studded sword
or striking with his brandished club
impassioned hunter of doves
once girls, he never hurts anyone.

This and lonely time for looking up
why these eyes are drawn, will dwell
on that aggressive constellation
to honour peace our love made
improbably invoke your presence
warm amongst cold, supposed gems
said to span a giant's waist

find new for you those three stars
Alnilam, Alnitak, Mintaka
beautiful, gentle, most loved.

## Changeling

What lost love does next with ravishing hair
cropping it boy-short, spiky and urchin
stunning, perhaps more feminine effect;
or letting it grow, a rich, impractical banner
nakedly asserting to the common gaze
luxuriant, her awesome sensuality:
whatever, it will be none of my business.

For me only memories of that changeling
a bold woman can become or is, physical
yet substantial as smoke, shape-shifting subtly
to be noticed in a frantic, headlong world
enchant both men and women in her sway
entwine forever forfeit heart of a lover
helpless, swimmer beyond his depth
and drowning in clutching, tangling kelp.

Even in our scant dreamy time, distinct styles:
shoulder-length with one purple strand
fashion shared with younger girlfriends;
a day of knowing she'd cut her hair, but
not saying: I'm a man; get these things wrong.

Best of all wonder at slender, intricate braids
worn over little ears for our anniversary
when none living, imagined, no actress
or catwalk model said to embody beauty
came within miles of her absolute loveliness;
no base jumper above Angel Falls or skydiver
stepping into space at twelve thousand feet
could be as infinitely, vibrantly alive
as my girl in that moment of our meeting:
glamour flooding into me at every pore
filling heart, lungs, guts and balls of a man
at adrenalin extremity, in a state of fugue.

To bring her head close to mine and trace
threads of near-blond, of auburn treasure
shades marking her bright place in nature
but sometimes drawn from a sly realm
of alchemy, Boots on wet Saturdays
glossy promises of tone, golden or copper:
she always flaunted a sheen of summer
tints of autumn to catch and keep light
floating freely over darker, deeper mystery.

Mostly, touching fay hair meant forgetting
warmth, weight, softness, so many qualities:
after all it only framed her dear face
needed constantly to be stroked back
from beloved brow by rapt, adoring hand.

She may give more time to another
but he can never know her completely
come to an end of entrancing changes
willed by herself, careless time, or simply
in turning and moving, by sunlight:
a consolation; no-one, claim what he will
could be more intimate than her poet
with, preternatural, each phase of her being.

## the fate of our familiars

because love builds as if by magic
a convoluted place of light, of shade
creates niches within new feeling
among hidden folds of its fabric
lovebirds of all kinds
made nests and courtly dances
reared gaping fluffy chicks
saw them safely take flight

elusive sharp-eyed mysteries
furred and fleeting
lined womb-dark little dens
with fine grasses or softer down
gave birth to small bundles
of pink tails tiny paws
licked and suckled them
till brilliant eyes opened
followed quivering noses
into a world of sight and scent
perfect copies of lithe parents

not knowing love could fail
and all it rears can fall
these charmed creatures
became suddenly homeless
gave various cries of despair
moved to my side of our ruin
where a few walls stubbornly stood
sheltered a lingering warmth
to sorrow and endure
in what was once a heart

## Falling star

West of a rising moon and mast-shaped, wheeling
winter constellation grave eyes turn to find
stars there re-named for you when my mind
was wandering, bereft; is one seen falling

through evening sky. Metal, manufactured speck
it catches failing light, leaves a long white trail
where, to change drab expectations, people sail
for the new world. We too rose above a wreck

of earlier hopes, made each other happy
planned an outdoor future full of sun – and shone.
But human lives are windblown leaves, get scattered

torn apart: like this worn heart trying sadly
to move on, act as if it never mattered
you once blazed across my sky and now you're gone.

## Other reasons

Why do painters stay patiently indoors
yet splash jubilant pigments on a canvas
across our minds? And poets make

a peculiar, intricate, almost magic
or perform with words mere conjuring tricks
anyone could do? To get the girl.
For an exalted girl, or sometimes a boy.

Since you're long gone and forever
won't listen to your fool repeating phrases
in a forgotten language, why do I write?

Sit inside when life sings in hot sun
be a flower where there are no bees
portray with inadequate, frangible colour
images of a perfection we've let fall?

No-one was ever more loved than you by me
I need to say so. But why should a world
steeped in stories of sadness and loss

care, if you can't? Find a pathos
particular to our doomed love?
I don't pretend to know: had to write
or go mad with grief. What else is there?

## from loss of heat

launched with a fanfare
twenty years ago
an almost forgotten NASA probe
now beyond   our tiny solar system

still orientating shiny panels
toward diminished
a starlike   cooling sun
faithfully returning facts
to mission control
an unsung back office

suddenly describes something new
a stream of particles
flying out from earth
to radiate   spread thinner   darken
going cold into deeper space

and two geeks in labcoats analyse
with open-mouthed amazement
one data-set after another
apply fine   and finer instruments
re-count rows of noughts
in each unlikely calculation
but come always to a conclusion
they state to their superiors

'it appears to be human tissue
probably some kind of muscle'

blown apart
heart that lost your heart

## taking her to Venice

she goes with me physically
catches my breath, waking
her flamelike nakedness first
moving into a busy morning
a little of her easy laughter
if i laugh, tossing burnt toast
or coffee let go cold
that sudden grin glimpsed
in my brief smile for another
slightly timid, brave brown eyes
somewhere back in blue
and occasionally her breasts
press within my chest
neat, stiffening nipples
tickling inside mine
or when my distracted hand
slides down a straight side
it still senses satin of her shape
and if lucky, unaware
for mindless happy moments
angles are poor impressions
of diminutive, her darling curves
and more rarely
a palm-shaped little mound
lifts, pushes urgently
part of that place in me
once-warmth wanting to flow
as under thrilled fingers
tongue, those last nights
and mornings i was young

## Hopeful blues

Somerset House has an airy Monet, 'Antibes 1888'
window through a London wall to southern splendour
a view across deep cobalt blue Gulf of Juan

west toward white scattered houses, a fishing village
Cannes – and inviting peaks of the Esterel
refracting heat madder-pink in solid sunlight.

Foreground a small, single pine, delicate and feathery

some shade in slight branches, down its dark flank.
Nothing could be simpler – sky beyond that pale
unmediated hue of human hope, continuing forever

into a glittering, but possible, touchable distance
exhilarating dazzle of Mediterranean summer.
Lucky twice over, having seen this masterpiece

and lazily wandered those hills, it's no secret:
without you, loveliness as art or reality isn't enough.
Henri Manguin painted my feeling: 'La sieste

Jeanne couchée sous les arbres', his dappled wife
nude and safe in nature, flushed skin warm stone
in texture, hair soft grass; uncomplicated joy

of baring oneself to sun's heat and a lover's eyes.

No sunshine or shade tree now, only tenderness
uprooted, severed, bleeding: yet mortal sorrow
can be overcome; to one day frame a picture

of hopeful blues and pinks again, fullness of life
love no less dear – courage you showed me. Till then
absence: of your naked, hot, approving gaze.

**naturalist**

birch leaves    new
beside a path we walked
bright as flame
green as a young heart
tell me spring has come
time to go back to work

it won't be easy
vivid wild pansies
nestle in warm dunes
as you once did with me
yellow of butterfly    purple
your coat on our anniversary
breathtaking    give delight
but    shine lonely eyes

lost jay feather
in a favourite wood
bluer than sky
soft as your hair
as your voice
when you lay in my arms
our beauty and nature's
not entangled
simply the same

fearless    these fragile leaves
and careless
sunthirsty flowers
spark another year
touch me
as they always have
and because

## Recanting

she went back to zero
and pretending, to placate him
made love out a liquid
– could be watered down
though such heady wine as her
resists all adulteration;

suggested feeling's lent
not given, that delicate aura
of timid forest creature
touching many, deeply
– her softness, solid currency
to be counted out and back:

as if our loving hadn't long
become iron in richer blood
– calcium of bones to a man
made sad, but so much stronger
hears an honest song of love
sustaining, real and true.

## for example

could i forget
dipping dark
shiny cherries slowly
by stiff
curving stalks
before tasting
them in silk of sighs
opened arching sex
a teasing touch
to please and spice
their tang
with yours?

**torn**

less often now
as life flows
in other channels
withdrawing from the landscape
in which we loved
my rueful mind
in its restless
turning of stones
feeble sifting of flotsam
sometimes uncovers gestures
she gave life to
or words she used
that delicate and brief
but definite
touch
like her lost caresses

she said when feeling low
not liking herself
losing faith in a courage
so clear to me
she used to re-read
my letters and their love
made her less harsh
self-critical

what would happen
if she was torn today
would words of mine
still sustain her?

i hope she'll never need them
and hope she always will

**true**

not a stream we're made to sit beside
while precious blood, heart's blood
clad as urchin hope, waif dreams
struggles, sinks or drifts out of reach;
we're in the swim and swept away:
glimpsing ourselves in mirrors
we see playthings to be toyed with
faces in other people's crowd

it flies and we fall to earth

yet one sunsoft, future summer day
we'll know time does not pass
it alters; even cherished feeling
we most want to think unchanged:
doesn't always mar, or fade
can cleanse a mind of posessive pain
smooth a face of longing and loss
to leave nothing; nothing but love

## Becoming

My elfin love will never die; though mortal
heartbroken, nor I. Stars unmoved, cold, shine on
each empty night, but I ached when she was gone
to be set free, not breathe...sadness, loss and all

deep human hurts of which we long to be healed.
Sea's always moody sea, restless yet ageless
its difference pulls on us fleeting, tailless
comets: our ripple in life's energy field

soon smoothed, absorbed in The Great Spirit we'll be
velvety face of new-born Spring's first flower
sap or sinew of a slim, aspiring tree.

There's only change of form: in time's endless stream
we'll part and mingle again. Winning's a dream
so's losing; we loved: became one forever.

## missed

beneath that other sun
he walked beside her
taller
calmer than before

arrived at timely moments
struck right notes
easily answered needs
his new confidence
restoring hers

under a different moon
and brighter stars
lay in slender arms

found strength unforeseen
a grace

through her
light-hearted
in the world of love
invulnerable

a good man who might
almost
have been taken for me

## coming home

when this world's
gentlest face
no longer fits, gets traded
for a newer model
yet to me your nearness
answers every need

you've climbed each peak
ambition once aspired to
turn from clamouring world
for calm, clear river of peace

in seasons beyond striving
where loving kindness
is almost all of life
and what matters so today
has no meaning

my softness become strength
we could be together

of course, you'll be old
grey and me almost a ghost
but while you beat

my heart, there'd be love

# MARTIN'S BOOK

"losing love is like a window in your heart
everybody sees you're blown apart"

– Paul Simon

## afterwards

imagine
faintly-lit emptiness
no star
larger or nearer
vastness of space

but glinting
silvery
a time capsule
stands out
against overwhelming cold
going on

bringing luminous memories
of a lost world
formula for happiness
essence of love

through nullity
to another sun
and orbiting planet
a human future

## Taking stock

Now, once simple screen
becomes quivering mosaic
yellow diamonds and orange
amongst familiar flakes of jade
With shivering siblings
spaced, isolated by human hands
this leaf-shaped birch
answers more integral force
flags up autumn
Time to count casualties of desire
in a rain and wind-thinned garden
nurtured and neglected by turns
soil of scant luck, where
too weary to break new ground
I scattered faint hopes
over a tangled plot
sometimes anguished at failing
of what was fragile
or galvanised by new shoots
and spurts of growth
Some are withered, others hale
but even strongest stems
knee-high to my need
surely seasons distant
across emptiness and ache
from heart-whole flower
and fruit of love

## i pulled

on a mountaining swell of years
had drained or evaporated meaning
your oceanic doubt
in mutual darkness, hard

my selfish, moon-blank pain, to you stunning
compelling, unimagined extreme
wrenched at a sinking heart
showed fearful, fathomless depths
where sodden, souls can drown

but married so long to contours
familiar, containing
retreating over rock and shifting sand
wave on wave, you chafed, fretted

never left your bed

## Nightwalk

Below us    a forever of sea
invisible now    still near and nagging
never silent    constantly breaking
beneath a path we're walking
solid ground
on which we hope our lives are built

Above    a permanence of cliffs
pale but distinct    dimly reflecting
finally arriving light
waiting    only to be fissured    fragment
wilfully fall on heads

Higher still    a chaos
and pattern of stars
cold lidless eyes    always staring down
fascinated or appalled

Wordless    we choose to walk
without a torch    sometimes stumbling
shins clutched at by skulking brambles
yet    precisely with our poor vision
groping senses
more completely part of dark
than bats that can hear sounds
not truly sounds    or glow-worms
greenish jewels against satin    gleaming
at measured intervals in long grass

Where we're edged out
round a bulking headland
what must be lighthouses    spark
out there    bright and sharp a second
far-off striking of matches

Turned to face inland
where cheerful-sounding streams
innocently   with relentless power
cut rock
darkness deepens
no light   colour   texture
only hint of human presence
this footworn groove   own heartbeats

We pass gaping openings
where sea comes even closer
and could choose   at ceaseless urging
of long-gestated hurt
or   on a momentary whim
to step sideways out of life
return our substance to stars
but   sometimes wondering why
keep walking

Alone with primal feeling
unaccepted selves
sudden owl calls
looming shapes of bears and wolves

## chink

beginning with blackness
unrelieved
wanting energy and courage
to make a clear point
go further
draw that sharp line

with putative horizon
divide night and day
or past from future
assert yourself, sustain
long enough
to vary dark with paler grey
a first hint of light
perhaps one muted star

abstracted, unsure
striving nonetheless
call this first sober image
'maybe'
learn to breathe again
take a step back
remember how to smile

**suture**

after sleep and returning to the wild
human, deep-exhaling storm
contained somehow in a single room
force of feeling lightning-clear
our pleasure naked as its beauty

free, you lay fused to my right side

covering intimately as snow
drifted, nestling and compacted
into loamy hollows between ribs
of enduring ridge, facing day
and melting hopes; another spring

## olympian

waking above painted waves
white-topped, silent, awed

dawn sun in breath-dewed window
simple as a child's drawing
yellow disc at blue
on darker-blue horizon

divides a fraught, mortal world
we'd forgotten, from love
our play-scented heaven

rays radiating behind you
scallop-shell to frame
a softer sheen, fragile but divine

slipped from ennobled arms
you stretch upwards, amaze
self-sculpted and possessed
large-hearted deity, littlest avatar

aphrodite rising
lissom from the foam

## Wrong

Earrings forgotten beside my bed
you went home midday Sunday
to feed loud cats
that have your nine-lived heart
came running, pressing
plaintively accusing
Saturday night's taxi promise broken

Liquid and seamless
held in a golden bowl, skin molten
base metal transmuted
knowing we made love
I wonder by what reverse alchemy
that's now not true
and melting words murmured
lip within lip
could cool with doubt

Tracing delicate loops of wire
touching small beads
become more definite
these mere things
than your body, or you

## dream home

no heirloom heavy with gilt
famous brands
pathetic ostentation
discovered love a diamond-sparkle
our glint of gold
good taste, music, food
feeling

anonymous mid-terrace
nothing special
but alive with easy laughter
a beaming child
happy in your lap and you in mine

air spiced with scent of flowers
breathing fronds
sun painting walls and furnishing
a cheerful space
hearth of bluer skies
brighter days

## hoping

                    a liminal
resinous scent, seeming exotic –
perhaps recognised as sandalwood
ribboning in a waking mind
where incense is never burned
till dispelled with a grimace
obliterated by morning routine

or in prosaic and everyday mode
solving problems, being practical
a shift to sweet abstraction
new voice intruding into monody
portal opened to another world
of frail, probably futile feeling
then noticed, suppressed with a sigh

seduction fallen for so easily
senses wanting to be lulled
slim, cool little dream-hand
slipped silently into larger
or slowly stroking, soothing brow

indulgence in fantasy or worse
a looking forward to
beginning of counting on
– hard, making a human heart
guard against its greatness

## but i do

and because i do
when you go, part of me

must also go, lonely child again
walking an empty corridor
intimidated by open doors –

to fall, from heaviness
into dark and cold
ache like ageing
beyond metaphor, simile
grieve like nothing but grief

or, learn to curl a lip
with a shrug, dismiss
friendship, tenderness and love
sacred feelings of the heart

– isn't it great to have choices?

**delicate**

not a round
glistening but blank one
telling nothing

or that half
horizon-tinged
we might set afloat
lemonslice
to jazz
our favourite drink

eyelash slender
newmade
this crescent moon is yours

underlooked easily
subtle nightshine
against sky still sunlit
otherness
almost mystical

curve hinting
world of high possibilities

mostly unseen slipping
calm
over day's throng
and dash
distinct
that shape of specialness
scientist or lunatic
might notice

or a lover

## not saying goodbye

perhaps one day to visit Paris
maybe not; make it deep
into his psyche and your own
leave our salty, shifting life
for bounded midlands

bearing unborn hope
away from this seaside world
today small and blue

a promise to be positive
letting me parody, eventually
your artful, sidelong smile
always darting somewhere
head in other clouds, dreams
friendships, a double future

distances you could travel
and never leave my heart

## taking flight

to be cold when i'm warm
face gales though here it's calm
but come through
at last into light
as i fall toward darkness
– where to fly on brave new wings
and always apart?

will you flow with weather
over sand and snow
silhouette far horizons
from searching
circle
finally return
splitting sun into liquid rays
seeing all colours
even my drab shade
part of one shining truth?

or must my wrong
reap your perfect right
keep us only to hemispheres
my dusk your dawn
our halves of sky?

**for Saousen**

whose love
keeps those cars in lane
vein into artery
as if they have somewhere to go
or lights windows of wan towers
where people toil
persuaded
a living can be earned
weep with men and women
for their frailty

must sometimes wander
leave a world of little gain
to turn alone in cluttered space
awhile unguarded

with tired eyes send a secret smile
that starts and sees another's need
held more than human
crowded conscience
falling away
feel wings beat in their blood

angel
lying down beside an angel

## opening

if new-born dew
on a breathing rose
you can receive
swelling, opening now
only from me, flows
behind your tired brow
soothing all its ache

a musky scent sinks deep
into groove and grain
of receptive memory
re-awakens sensual feeling
dissolves stresses into calm

and delicious satin
of its smoke-soft petals
under slowed
relaxing fingers
or touching your smoothed face
is cool as were pillows
and easy sleep of childhood
there's no worry, doubt, loss
for a while, anyway

but this bloom exists
only in a loving voice
speaking softly though urgent
close to a small ear
dense warmth of tight dark hair
flower-aura
of your open-hearted face

will you still tell me
i have nothing to give you?

**trusting**

1

sleeping
your face on a pillow
naked and helpless
but smooth
relaxed

i look down
at half-moons
of your eyelids
lashes distinct
as rays of light

almost cartoon-like
betty boop
their power to move me

2

hollowed
feeling guilty
not as good to you
as i mean to be

a child
struggling
with someone stronger
my fingers are bent back
things twisted
out of my grasp

strange
how caring too much
gets in our way
makes distances
i must learn from this
stop running

3

now you're smiling
lifting arms to me
and i fall into you
can't resist
a pull of gravity
desire

when you can trust me
awake
as you do asleep
when my back is straight
this mind clear
perhaps
i'll accept
me
as easily as you do

## Virago

You're that woman: so feminine in yielding
too easily and long for others' need, but
someone besides in sensuous, fertile poems
that sperm-like, swim tenaciously
probing moist folds of opening minds
seeking earned, elusive receptivity;
electro-chemical impulses to animate
common circuitry for memory and desire.

Your lyrics, fish with lungs and eel-slick
able to leave water, better than survive;
embers that, wilfully leaping from a fire
look to nestle in desiccated fibres
of editorial indifference and smoulder
finally set smug, a narrow place ablaze:
molecular, organic, they'll make their way
avid to radiate, connect, create new life.

# Life study

To my left a padlock set in purple
and right the key, explored by feelers
of a might-be mollusc; symbols
displaced from outer-day reality
their mystery unmitigated

Creating her own space and a sparse
field of stars, she invents constellations
sprawling human figures
scored quickly into blackness

Nearby, Venetian carnival masks
female an outline, muted;
male plumed and peacock-proud
border magnified words
a poem glimpsed through water

Ivy-leaves limpid, ink on paper
some pendent from plain stalks
or simplified, revealing other forms:
seeing things differently, again
she moulds and frames, moves
intent, between pools of sunlight

Awed, I'll leave strands of seaweed
by her door, or a bold iris
gold-dust in its throat, hoping
shape will be captured, colour held
vivid; a gesture live forever

## La Gioconda

Slip beside me down a stream of light
welling at the core of a blazing building
sun-defined pyramid, amazingly congruous
brilliantly poised at this airy slant
to surroundings weighted with tradition
a crowded, grandiose, old-fashioned place
emphatically modern and alive

Let's weave through murmurous galleries
of garishly-dressed people who gaze
at dowdy portraits staring stiffly back
dull landscapes that never come to life
but we can go beyond what's dust
slalom round sharp, skilled elbows
stand stilled before moving Mona Lisa

Familiar, unfaded Florentine woman
framed in misty, imagined Italian hills
for five centuries she's made admirers
has her power, an irresistible something
found so often in a perfect stranger
yet after iconic status, over-exposure
seems endearingly small and pale

It won't diminish her mystery and grace
if I blurt clumsy, passionate contrasts
between a two-dimensional delicacy
that famously equivocal expression
of hinted, arguable, fabled tenderness
and your face, these tangible contours
active and changeable as weather

Breathing and touching is beauty
as pensive Lisa no doubt once knew
this physicality our chance to create
with a brush of lips, bravura colour
paint a fauve picture of such feeling
we'll make a flagrant masterpiece
shared horizon open as your smile

## Outside time

No taller than us and our emotion
slender, very young
skin smooth and pliant
without marks of amputation
but a strange tree

Clearly deciduous, partner to warmth
a million green leaves
heart-shaped, light-seeking
reminding us where love stands

Full summer in January
brave discrepancy, vulnerable to fire
of frost, it trembles

## long distance

no more
when gaps lengthen
and each comes from farther away
as if passing under oceans
threaded awkwardly between mountains
a line crackles more
though it doesn't
or your voice is growing smaller

local accent becoming alien
disembodied, a siberian dialect
chill inflections we're slowly absorbing

losing our low notes
bass warm and earthy
a range that inclined
to irreverent humour, honest lust

where once we confided
caressed without touching
no more
till you're real again
language beyond words

## not luck

or its absence, not quite
clumsiness, lack of self-confidence
though familiar aspects
palms that didn't sweat
till just before you had to shake hands

or having every answer at an interview
but wrong tie, holding yourself
upright, in a sharp suit
still a monkey

ringing too early, too late – too often
seeming pushy and crass, losing it
when to win was play it cool

finding good words, true words
but not the right words
knowing what you should have said
only later, alone

in front of a mirror
you wake to each day
seeing in a weather-beaten face
what it means to live without grace

## Known fact

In sweaty summer Munich
freedom is a golden angel
poised on a pedestal
arms upraised
over river, city and people
aloof

Trying to frame her glitter
and his girlfriend
in one photo
a lucky man
failed to find an angle
gave it up
focused on his lover

And felt what he'd done
smiled
lowering the camera
stepped forward
eagerly kissed
with whom to be free
better far than gold or angels
a living girl

## August night at the Monkey Café

Sweet-smelling air, thickened, sticky
throbs, barely gaseous
our throats and nostrils clagged
we lean back, mould ourselves to music
eyes closed to dreadlocks, tattoos
nose-rings glinting

Tall kelp under rolling sea, a circuit
of singleted drummers sway
put shoulders into sweating tom-toms
or tap sparingly at sharp-sounding tablas
as a candle-dim room comes loose
from floor, ceiling, bricks and mortar
its own distinct vibration, easing mind
body, nothing real beyond itself

Slow, but seance-definite
gripped by bass rhythm, your wine glass
moves, marches across a table
trails shivering splashes till rescued
then you smile, touch my hip

Sometimes starting to lose shape
or falter, beat flirts with a breakdown
but lifted heads grin, nod and hands blur
compress, re-sculpt solid air
steady, set a new pattern
while in a night-blue panel, one small
smoky window, painted stars unnoticed
go round a crescent moon

Outside, dazed by oxygen and deaf
own voices seeming strange to us
heading for a taxi, arms linked and minds
laughing at everything, nothing
know we've found something good
felt it's first tempo

**if**

      this mildest, merest man
who never waved a magic wand
prayed, or called on occult powers
surrounded you with suddenly
a glamour of jungle fragrances
potent, jangling more-than-perfume
carried far on leaf-broken light
and pacific-heavy, humid air;

or found song to fill a wintry room
nightingale phrases of summer birds
perhaps not rare, but rarely heard
each rising descant true to you
and real as a fluttered heart;

or lazily drizzled onto your tongue
a lemon cinnamon honey tang
sweet as childhood pilfered sugar
salt of pungent, rumoured foods
from baking, bronzy eastern lands;

or suspended, brought to shimmer
before so wide, your startled eyes
with his fay sheen, a hummingbird
untold wealth of satin purple
treasure-trove of silken green;

or buried you alive in arctic snow
stunned by overwhelming heat
and hug of fanged, of all fiercest
a gentlest mother giving suck
to cherished cub, baby polar bear
could you be surprised to say
what common senses let you see
it's special to be loved by me?

## Eye candy

Profuse detail in landscape design
living tinsel to festive minds
that, in comfortable, median seasons
process each serviceable kind of green

Power stations, but 'renewables'
factories making sugar and oxygen
turning insects into baby birds
shrews to cats
farm animals into us
having sustained all stomachs
begin to fall

Random or wilful in sequence
and resultant pattern snapshots:
one giving itself easily
twisting free in a sudden gust and slow
teasing coming to earth
another stubborn, clinging
to existence without purpose

Leaves before our eyes trance-lucent
saturated by last warming sun
hoarding citrus shades
most beautiful now
waiting to drop, dead
gorgeous

## learning

calmly to think it
a narrow canvas
mostly drab
substrate
formless and cloudy
to filaments
and flickering energies

string and beads
highlights flame-coloured
turning deepest blue
green-eyed
cooling
grey as ashes
blood-red going rosy

intersecting
entwining others
obscured passing under
through
or standing proud
predominant as rays
and sequin stars
sewn on dark ground

certainly
as something worked
if not made
a potential
place to design
adorn even plainest cloth

## To a magician

Most amazing is cool morning air
bemusing freshness on foreheads
and under Russian-doll toes as barefoot
bareheaded you cross a terrace
that, broiled hours from now
will shimmer with stunning heat

In big fluffy dressing gowns
breakfasting on our own balcony
leaning into flavour, aroma of romance
table decorated with cut flowers
coffee, fruit, two croissants
food sweet and light for a hot lazy day

Insular, carefree Corfu summer
dazzling walls of new whitewash
quick lizards brazenly basking
trees gnarled, sagging, skirted
with nets to gather olives
butterflies floating from gloom into glare
omnipresent sun already high
lighting landscapes with sure artistry
succulent colour, tactile shadow

Perhaps you'll wear a wide-brimmed hat
shades of a reclusive movie star
chic little clinging top
loose harem trousers totally you
jaunty, feminine, exciting

We'll wander down town's one street
toward brilliant, bird-calling sea
cross a reedy, glitter stream
home to snakes and terrapins
curly-headed boys on motorbikes
wolf-whistling, waving at you
older men nodding respect to me
for this marvellous woman I'm with

Grinning my most buccaneering grin
certain you couldn't be more beautiful
if your name was Aphrodite
and locals garlanded your hair
with green leaves, with roses
offered bread and wine
called you their goddess

To laugh aloud, linger by shore's
strong tang of salt in spread nets
upturned keels of fishing boats
staring eyes for luck painted on bows
my heart leaping, leaning to lick
and kiss dripped ice cream
from beside your parted lips

Sky another ocean behind dazed heads
liquid sunlight sticky on our brows
we climb to an ancient castle wall
feel vague, refreshing hints of breeze
above fabulous Kassiopi
where we face over an inky-blue strait
near, mysterious Albania, seeming empty
unspoilt, white as her name
agree no view's more lovely

*

Much later, loll beneath broad stripes
translucent canopy of a pavement Café
splash chilled water on necks cooked raw
drain a glass of colourful and cold
write joky postcards home, saying
'wish you were here'
not meaning it for a second

Sun relenting, sinking into stone
pink-tinged, rugged, drowsing bulk
of broad-shouldered Pandokrator
day drifting west while we sit and dream
evening soon in woodsmoke-scented east
as sea and sky vie to be deepest blue
sea winning easily, sky responding
with huge and clear, a star
soon millions more as consolation

Over dinner and a devastating drink
of fermented grape juice
knowing we achieved nothing today
and feeling great
I can only smile, squeeze your hands
no words wild enough
to convey this crazy happiness
magic you make
without gesture or incantation
because, in a face soft-lit
by tremulous sea-borne moonlight
you see beyond me my best self

Returning on rising, falling paths
parting waves of lank grass
crested with a night-sea glint
greenish tiny lanterns of glow-worms
between brashly-lit buildings
and noisier celebrations
we'll lie naked together on a bed
skin beaded, glistening
liking what we see, but for now
too languid to make love
except with our eyes

# Nirvana

Perfect as gut stretched over gape
wires taut over fret and nothing
but a box, projecting ribbons
streaming colour down grey streets

To those rootless, wandering
kin and companion, partner-shaped
held, rocked gently between hips
caressed at neck and waist
strings soul-deep, resonant, warm
cool clarity of horns, percussion
a river of emotion, whole orchestra

More than human voice, telling
truths of failing, little victories
someone else's story also ours
able finally to loose a flood
tears long held in, let them go
lift from loss into laughter

Not to possess or even play
but be a guitar: brought to light
delight, made a fuss and focus of
stroked till cat-like, purring
give pleasure and be loved

## Funny valentine

Sultry nights ago, in starry still and hush
at restless boundary between alien worlds
a miracle recurred; then, over signs
waves passed, left sand, sun-pressed, smooth
nothing but miles of towels, tanned skin.

Now small patches sink, become pitted
tiny heads raised, oval eyes peering
dark, unpupilled; pausing, no signal yet
scenting their element so far away
baby turtles draw on last egg-yolk energy
for the dash to face their life, adventure.

A demon screams down that beach, his arms
windmilling to ward off gulls, stamping
scaring crabs back into burrows; or calmer

carrying dozens to sea, till delirious.
However foolish, wants each adorable atom
to have its chance; you to accept a man
so sentimental, the gentle to win for once.

## loving

human beings
knowing themselves
to be fearful
clumsy
self-absorbed

choose
to step out
on a slender
trembling
scary tightrope

stretching away
further
than eyes can see
its other end
invisible

in a fog
beyond
a gaping chasm
over which
they must walk

balancing
only with hope
and faith
outstretched hands
with love

counting
on another
fearful
and clumsy
just like them

## Apfelbaum 1 (Gustav Klimt 1912. Österreichische Galerie Belvedere, Vienna)

Orbing sunlight into sugar tang
fruit orange-red against green-white
proudly new-laden, Klimt's small, young
first apple tree can root and lift us

Eve might come here leading Adam
by a longing keen, but not longing
for which there isn't yet a word:
sensation too sole, naive, throbbing
in a heart man didn't know he had
to be named desire
or bring anything but delight

All things in unselfconscious minds
paint-bright as these eager faces
this crowd scene of real flowers:
dandelion, daisy, long-rayed alpine asters
a floating clan of composite beauty
butterflies tethered at grass tops

An untasted freshness
those apples would also have for us
could we reach up and pick one:
no chatty snake ever to insinuate
seductive pain of shading knowledge
disharmony of driven movement
exile to futures and mortality

Our expulsion overturned by art
we walk again in paradise, unblemished
felt cool and crisp beneath bare feet

## Way of the road

Everyone on a strange road
trying to read signs
fading when first seen
unsure where they're going
which way to turn
or sighting a landmark
lucky enough
to be on that right track
We happened to meet
slowing on a long uphill slog
a couple of ragged runners
panting along together
pleased to have company
share a few laughs
lash this low terrain
Dogs bark at us
some people stare coldly
cars speed to spatter mud
and it feels good
that someone's there
But it doesn't mean
you must run at my pace
or I'll always stay
breathless beside you
When it's time
to accelerate or turn
we'll smile and wave
go on alone

## stars

too often supporting actors
gunned down resisting bad guys
or carried off by a plastic shark
we've stood half-shadowed
while spotlight fell on others
neglected crying needs
to play lesser roles

wasted on hollywooden remakes
we'll improvise an original
head a towering cast
become larger than life
snap a stretched budget
choosing costumes, locations
i'll compose a soundtrack
you can sing the hit

through losing, finding
canned smoke and sub-plots
to suddenly see clearly
not afraid or hungry
like people on tv
we're together, strong

our movie, you and me up there
in a pool of light, laughing
totally alive and ten feet tall
avant garde, no script
everything possible

94

***You***

*Crowded and hurried, dazzled by cosmetic*
*glamour, people might not notice your soft face*
*in a crowd. As many blindly pass a place*
*where some shy little wildflower does the trick*

*of stopping time, heartbeat and breath a moment*
*in awe at fragile yet vivid, bold beauty*
*they'd rush on unaware. But I was lucky*
*saw your specialness so clearly, you couldn't*

*hide such tender, distinct glory from these eyes*
*that window a soul of learning and longing.*
*A conservationist, trained in protecting*

*but adoring what's wild, delicate, brave, free*
*knowing you're truly lovely: I can't disguise*
*hope you'll look deeply, find a like grace in me.*

**Martin J. White** was born in Winchester, Hampshire and lived in Yorkshire and London before settling in Swansea in October 1992.

A conservationist, he has carried out many surveys on butterflies and moths in the region and is currently South Wales branch organiser for the charity Butterfly Conservation and a voluntary warden for Cyngor Cefn Gwlad Cymru, the Countryside Council for Wales. Among other achievements, he discovered two moth species completely new to Wales. He is also a familiar figure on the streets of Swansea as a campaigner against health service cuts, for free education and on other issues.

After working as a songwriter in London, Martin turned to poetry in Yorkshire in the late 1980s, attending a weekly workshop in Huddersfield with poets including Milner Place and occasionally, Simon Armitage. He has had poems published in a number of anthologies and such magazines as *The Echo Room*, *Orbis*, *Iota*, *Weyfarers* and *Poetry Wales*.

Martin has always said 'if I could have my life again, I'd like to be a painter' but after visiting the modern art galleries of Munich, Vienna and Venice in the summer of 2004, he began producing images such as the one (entitled 'skies she wears') for the cover of this book.

The author would be pleased to receive feedback about these poems at:
21 Highmoor, Maritime Quarter, Swansea, SA1 1YE
Tel: 01792 477984